DATE:_____

INSTRUCTOR:_____

TRAINING PARTNERS:_____

SESSION GOAL:_____

TECHNIQUE 1

_____

_____

TECHNIQUE 2

_____

_____

TECHNIQUE 3

_____

_____

NOTES

_____

_____

HOURS TRAINED:_____

DATE:_____ BELT RANK:_____

INSTRUCTOR:_____ WEIGHT:_____

TRAINING PARTNERS:_____

SESSION GOAL:_____

TECHNIQUE 1

_____

_____

TECHNIQUE 2

_____

_____

TECHNIQUE 3

_____

_____

NOTES

_____

_____

HOURS TRAINED:_____

DATE:_____ BELT RANK:_____

INSTRUCTOR:_____ WEIGHT:_____

TRAINING PARTNERS:_____

SESSION GOAL:_____

TECHNIQUE 1

_____

_____

TECHNIQUE 2

_____

_____

TECHNIQUE 3

_____

_____

NOTES

_____

_____

HOURS TRAINED:_____

DATE:_____ BELT RANK:_____

INSTRUCTOR:_____ WEIGHT:_____

TRAINING PARTNERS:_____

SESSION GOAL:_____

TECHNIQUE 1

_____

_____

TECHNIQUE 2

_____

_____

TECHNIQUE 3

_____

_____

NOTES

_____

_____

HOURS TRAINED:_____

DATE:_____ BELT RANK:_____

INSTRUCTOR:_____ WEIGHT:_____

TRAINING PARTNERS:_____

SESSION GOAL:_____

TECHNIQUE 1

_____

_____

TECHNIQUE 2

_____

_____

TECHNIQUE 3

_____

_____

NOTES

_____

_____

HOURS TRAINED:_____

DATE:_____ BELT RANK:_____

INSTRUCTOR:_____ WEIGHT:_____

TRAINING PARTNERS:_____

SESSION GOAL:_____

TECHNIQUE 1

_____
_____

TECHNIQUE 2

_____
_____

TECHNIQUE 3

_____
_____

NOTES

_____
_____

HOURS TRAINED:_____

DATE:_____ BELT RANK:_____

INSTRUCTOR:_____ WEIGHT:_____

TRAINING PARTNERS:_____

SESSION GOAL:_____

TECHNIQUE 1

_____
_____

TECHNIQUE 2

_____
_____

TECHNIQUE 3

_____
_____

NOTES

_____
_____

HOURS TRAINED:_____

DATE:_____ BELT RANK:_____

INSTRUCTOR:_____ WEIGHT:_____

TRAINING PARTNERS:_____

SESSION GOAL:_____

TECHNIQUE 1

_____

_____

TECHNIQUE 2

_____

_____

TECHNIQUE 3

_____

_____

NOTES

_____

_____

HOURS TRAINED:_____

DATE:_____ BELT RANK:_____

INSTRUCTOR:_____ WEIGHT:_____

TRAINING PARTNERS:_____

SESSION GOAL:_____

TECHNIQUE 1

_____

_____

TECHNIQUE 2

_____

_____

TECHNIQUE 3

_____

_____

NOTES

_____

_____

HOURS TRAINED:_____

DATE:_____ BELT RANK:_____

INSTRUCTOR:_____ WEIGHT:_____

TRAINING PARTNERS:_____

SESSION GOAL:_____

TECHNIQUE 1

_____

_____

TECHNIQUE 2

_____

_____

TECHNIQUE 3

_____

_____

NOTES

_____

_____

HOURS TRAINED:_____

DATE:_____ BELT RANK:_____

INSTRUCTOR:_____ WEIGHT:_____

TRAINING PARTNERS:_____

SESSION GOAL:_____

TECHNIQUE 1

_____

_____

TECHNIQUE 2

_____

_____

TECHNIQUE 3

_____

_____

NOTES

_____

_____

HOURS TRAINED:_____

DATE:_____ BELT RANK:_____

INSTRUCTOR:_____ WEIGHT:_____

TRAINING PARTNERS:_____

SESSION GOAL:_____

TECHNIQUE 1

_____
_____

TECHNIQUE 2

_____
_____

TECHNIQUE 3

_____
_____

NOTES

_____
_____

HOURS TRAINED:_____

DATE:_____ BELT RANK:_____

INSTRUCTOR:_____ WEIGHT:_____

TRAINING PARTNERS:_____

SESSION GOAL:_____

TECHNIQUE 1

_____
_____

TECHNIQUE 2

_____
_____

TECHNIQUE 3

_____
_____

NOTES

_____
_____

HOURS TRAINED:_____

DATE:_____ BELT RANK:_____

INSTRUCTOR:_____ WEIGHT:_____

TRAINING PARTNERS:_____

SESSION GOAL:_____

TECHNIQUE 1

_____

_____

TECHNIQUE 2

_____

_____

TECHNIQUE 3

_____

_____

NOTES

_____

_____

HOURS TRAINED:_____

DATE:_____ BELT RANK:_____

INSTRUCTOR:_____ WEIGHT:_____

TRAINING PARTNERS:_____

SESSION GOAL:_____

TECHNIQUE 1

_____
_____

TECHNIQUE 2

_____
_____

TECHNIQUE 3

_____
_____

NOTES

_____
_____

HOURS TRAINED:_____

DATE:_____ BELT RANK:_____

INSTRUCTOR:_____ WEIGHT:_____

TRAINING PARTNERS:_____

SESSION GOAL:_____

TECHNIQUE 1

_____

_____

TECHNIQUE 2

_____

_____

TECHNIQUE 3

_____

_____

NOTES

_____

_____

HOURS TRAINED:_____

DATE:_____ BELT RANK:_____

INSTRUCTOR:_____ WEIGHT:_____

TRAINING PARTNERS:_____

SESSION GOAL:_____

TECHNIQUE 1

_____

_____

TECHNIQUE 2

_____

_____

TECHNIQUE 3

_____

_____

NOTES

_____

_____

HOURS TRAINED:_____

DATE:_____ BELT RANK:_____

INSTRUCTOR:_____ WEIGHT:_____

TRAINING PARTNERS:_____

SESSION GOAL:_____

TECHNIQUE 1

_____

_____

TECHNIQUE 2

_____

_____

TECHNIQUE 3

_____

_____

NOTES

_____

_____

HOURS TRAINED:_____

DATE:_____ BELT RANK:_____

INSTRUCTOR:_____ WEIGHT:_____

TRAINING PARTNERS:_____

SESSION GOAL:_____

TECHNIQUE 1

_____

_____

TECHNIQUE 2

_____

_____

TECHNIQUE 3

_____

_____

NOTES

_____

_____

HOURS TRAINED:_____

DATE:_____ BELT RANK:_____

INSTRUCTOR:_____ WEIGHT:_____

TRAINING PARTNERS:_____

SESSION GOAL:_____

TECHNIQUE 1

_____

_____

TECHNIQUE 2

_____

_____

TECHNIQUE 3

_____

_____

NOTES

_____

_____

HOURS TRAINED:_____

DATE:_____ BELT RANK:_____

INSTRUCTOR:_____ WEIGHT:_____

TRAINING PARTNERS:_____

SESSION GOAL:_____

TECHNIQUE 1

_____
_____

TECHNIQUE 2

_____
_____

TECHNIQUE 3

_____
_____

NOTES

_____
_____

HOURS TRAINED:_____

DATE:_____ BELT RANK:_____

INSTRUCTOR:_____ WEIGHT:_____

TRAINING PARTNERS:_____

SESSION GOAL:_____

TECHNIQUE 1

_____

_____

TECHNIQUE 2

_____

_____

TECHNIQUE 3

_____

_____

NOTES

_____

_____

HOURS TRAINED:_____

DATE:_____ BELT RANK:_____

INSTRUCTOR:_____ WEIGHT:_____

TRAINING PARTNERS:_____

SESSION GOAL:_____

TECHNIQUE 1

_____

_____

TECHNIQUE 2

_____

_____

TECHNIQUE 3

_____

_____

NOTES

_____

_____

HOURS TRAINED:_____

DATE:_____ BELT RANK:_____

INSTRUCTOR:_____ WEIGHT:_____

TRAINING PARTNERS:_____

SESSION GOAL:_____

TECHNIQUE 1

_____
_____

TECHNIQUE 2

_____
_____

TECHNIQUE 3

_____
_____

NOTES

_____
_____

HOURS TRAINED:_____

DATE:_____ BELT RANK:_____

INSTRUCTOR:_____ WEIGHT:_____

TRAINING PARTNERS:_____

SESSION GOAL:_____

TECHNIQUE 1

_____

_____

TECHNIQUE 2

_____

_____

TECHNIQUE 3

_____

_____

NOTES

_____

_____

HOURS TRAINED:_____

DATE:_____ BELT RANK:_____

INSTRUCTOR:_____ WEIGHT:_____

TRAINING PARTNERS:_____

SESSION GOAL:_____

TECHNIQUE 1

_____
_____

TECHNIQUE 2

_____
_____

TECHNIQUE 3

_____
_____

NOTES

_____
_____

HOURS TRAINED:_____

DATE:_____ BELT RANK:_____

INSTRUCTOR:_____ WEIGHT:_____

TRAINING PARTNERS:_____

SESSION GOAL:_____

TECHNIQUE 1

_____

_____

TECHNIQUE 2

_____

_____

TECHNIQUE 3

_____

_____

NOTES

_____

_____

HOURS TRAINED:_____

DATE:_____ BELT RANK:_____

INSTRUCTOR:_____ WEIGHT:_____

TRAINING PARTNERS:_____

SESSION GOAL:_____

TECHNIQUE 1

_____

_____

TECHNIQUE 2

_____

_____

TECHNIQUE 3

_____

_____

NOTES

_____

_____

HOURS TRAINED:_____

DATE:_____ BELT RANK:_____

INSTRUCTOR:_____ WEIGHT:_____

TRAINING PARTNERS:_____

SESSION GOAL:_____

TECHNIQUE 1

_____

_____

TECHNIQUE 2

_____

_____

TECHNIQUE 3

_____

_____

NOTES

_____

_____

HOURS TRAINED:_____

DATE:_____ BELT RANK:_____

INSTRUCTOR:_____ WEIGHT:_____

TRAINING PARTNERS:_____

SESSION GOAL:_____

TECHNIQUE 1

_____
_____

TECHNIQUE 2

_____
_____

TECHNIQUE 3

_____
_____

NOTES

_____
_____

HOURS TRAINED:_____

DATE:_____ BELT RANK:_____

INSTRUCTOR:_____ WEIGHT:_____

TRAINING PARTNERS:_____

SESSION GOAL:_____

TECHNIQUE 1

_____
_____

TECHNIQUE 2

_____
_____

TECHNIQUE 3

_____
_____

NOTES

_____
_____

HOURS TRAINED:_____

DATE:_____ BELT RANK:_____

INSTRUCTOR:_____ WEIGHT:_____

TRAINING PARTNERS:_____

SESSION GOAL:_____

TECHNIQUE 1

_____

_____

TECHNIQUE 2

_____

_____

TECHNIQUE 3

_____

_____

NOTES

_____

_____

HOURS TRAINED:_____

DATE:_____ BELT RANK:_____

INSTRUCTOR:_____ WEIGHT:_____

TRAINING PARTNERS:_____

SESSION GOAL:_____

TECHNIQUE 1

_____

_____

TECHNIQUE 2

_____

_____

TECHNIQUE 3

_____

_____

NOTES

_____

_____

HOURS TRAINED:_____

DATE:_____ BELT RANK:_____

INSTRUCTOR:_____ WEIGHT:_____

TRAINING PARTNERS:_____

SESSION GOAL:_____

TECHNIQUE 1

_____
_____

TECHNIQUE 2

_____
_____

TECHNIQUE 3

_____
_____

NOTES

_____
_____

HOURS TRAINED:_____

DATE:_____ BELT RANK:_____

INSTRUCTOR:_____ WEIGHT:_____

TRAINING PARTNERS:_____

SESSION GOAL:_____

TECHNIQUE 1

_____

_____

TECHNIQUE 2

_____

_____

TECHNIQUE 3

_____

_____

NOTES

_____

_____

HOURS TRAINED:_____

DATE:_____ BELT RANK:_____

INSTRUCTOR:_____ WEIGHT:_____

TRAINING PARTNERS:_____

SESSION GOAL:_____

TECHNIQUE 1

_____

_____

TECHNIQUE 2

_____

_____

TECHNIQUE 3

_____

_____

NOTES

_____

_____

HOURS TRAINED:_____

DATE:_____ BELT RANK:_____

INSTRUCTOR:_____ WEIGHT:_____

TRAINING PARTNERS:_____

SESSION GOAL:_____

TECHNIQUE 1

_____
_____

TECHNIQUE 2

_____
_____

TECHNIQUE 3

_____
_____

NOTES

_____
_____

HOURS TRAINED:_____

DATE:_____ BELT RANK:_____

INSTRUCTOR:_____ WEIGHT:_____

TRAINING PARTNERS:_____

SESSION GOAL:_____

TECHNIQUE 1

_____

_____

TECHNIQUE 2

_____

_____

TECHNIQUE 3

_____

_____

NOTES

_____

_____

HOURS TRAINED:_____

DATE:_____ BELT RANK:_____

INSTRUCTOR:_____ WEIGHT:_____

TRAINING PARTNERS:_____

SESSION GOAL:_____

TECHNIQUE 1

_____
_____

TECHNIQUE 2

_____
_____

TECHNIQUE 3

_____
_____

NOTES

_____
_____

HOURS TRAINED:_____

DATE:_____ BELT RANK:_____

INSTRUCTOR:_____ WEIGHT:_____

TRAINING PARTNERS:_____

SESSION GOAL:_____

TECHNIQUE 1

_____

_____

TECHNIQUE 2

_____

_____

TECHNIQUE 3

_____

_____

NOTES

_____

_____

HOURS TRAINED:_____

DATE:_____ BELT RANK:_____

INSTRUCTOR:_____ WEIGHT:_____

TRAINING PARTNERS:_____

SESSION GOAL:_____

TECHNIQUE 1

_____

_____

TECHNIQUE 2

_____

_____

TECHNIQUE 3

_____

_____

NOTES

_____

_____

HOURS TRAINED:_____

DATE:_____ BELT RANK:_____

INSTRUCTOR:_____ WEIGHT:_____

TRAINING PARTNERS:_____

SESSION GOAL:_____

TECHNIQUE 1

_____
_____

TECHNIQUE 2

_____
_____

TECHNIQUE 3

_____
_____

NOTES

_____
_____

HOURS TRAINED:_____

DATE:_____ BELT RANK:_____

INSTRUCTOR:_____ WEIGHT:_____

TRAINING PARTNERS:_____

SESSION GOAL:_____

TECHNIQUE 1

_____

_____

TECHNIQUE 2

_____

_____

TECHNIQUE 3

_____

_____

NOTES

_____

_____

HOURS TRAINED:_____

DATE:_____ BELT RANK:_____

INSTRUCTOR:_____ WEIGHT:_____

TRAINING PARTNERS:_____

SESSION GOAL:_____

TECHNIQUE 1

_____

_____

TECHNIQUE 2

_____

_____

TECHNIQUE 3

_____

_____

NOTES

_____

_____

HOURS TRAINED:_____

DATE:_____ BELT RANK:_____

INSTRUCTOR:_____ WEIGHT:_____

TRAINING PARTNERS:_____

SESSION GOAL:_____

TECHNIQUE 1

_____
_____

TECHNIQUE 2

_____
_____

TECHNIQUE 3

_____
_____

NOTES

_____
_____

HOURS TRAINED:_____

DATE:_____ BELT RANK:_____

INSTRUCTOR:_____ WEIGHT:_____

TRAINING PARTNERS:_____

SESSION GOAL:_____

TECHNIQUE 1

_____

_____

TECHNIQUE 2

_____

_____

TECHNIQUE 3

_____

_____

NOTES

_____

_____

HOURS TRAINED:_____

DATE:_____ BELT RANK:_____

INSTRUCTOR:_____ WEIGHT:_____

TRAINING PARTNERS:_____

SESSION GOAL:_____

TECHNIQUE 1

_____

_____

TECHNIQUE 2

_____

_____

TECHNIQUE 3

_____

_____

NOTES

_____

_____

HOURS TRAINED:_____

DATE:_____ BELT RANK:_____

INSTRUCTOR:_____ WEIGHT:_____

TRAINING PARTNERS:_____

SESSION GOAL:_____

TECHNIQUE 1

_____
_____
_____

TECHNIQUE 2

_____
_____
_____

TECHNIQUE 3

_____
_____
_____

NOTES

_____
_____
_____

HOURS TRAINED:_____

DATE:_____ BELT RANK:_____

INSTRUCTOR:_____ WEIGHT:_____

TRAINING PARTNERS:_____

SESSION GOAL:_____

TECHNIQUE 1

_____

_____

TECHNIQUE 2

_____

_____

TECHNIQUE 3

_____

_____

NOTES

_____

_____

HOURS TRAINED:_____

DATE:_____ BELT RANK:_____

INSTRUCTOR:_____ WEIGHT:_____

TRAINING PARTNERS:_____

SESSION GOAL:_____

TECHNIQUE 1

_____
_____

TECHNIQUE 2

_____
_____

TECHNIQUE 3

_____
_____

NOTES

_____
_____

HOURS TRAINED:_____

DATE:_____ BELT RANK:_____

INSTRUCTOR:_____ WEIGHT:_____

TRAINING PARTNERS:_____

SESSION GOAL:_____

TECHNIQUE 1

_____
_____

TECHNIQUE 2

_____
_____

TECHNIQUE 3

_____
_____

NOTES

_____
_____

HOURS TRAINED:_____

DATE:_____ BELT RANK:_____

INSTRUCTOR:_____ WEIGHT:_____

TRAINING PARTNERS:_____

SESSION GOAL:_____

TECHNIQUE 1

_____

_____

TECHNIQUE 2

_____

_____

TECHNIQUE 3

_____

_____

NOTES

_____

_____

HOURS TRAINED:_____

DATE:_____ BELT RANK:_____

INSTRUCTOR:_____ WEIGHT:_____

TRAINING PARTNERS:_____

SESSION GOAL:_____

TECHNIQUE 1

_____
_____

TECHNIQUE 2

_____
_____

TECHNIQUE 3

_____
_____

NOTES

_____
_____

HOURS TRAINED:_____

DATE:_____ BELT RANK:_____

INSTRUCTOR:_____ WEIGHT:_____

TRAINING PARTNERS:_____

SESSION GOAL:_____

TECHNIQUE 1

_____

_____

TECHNIQUE 2

_____

_____

TECHNIQUE 3

_____

_____

NOTES

_____

_____

HOURS TRAINED:_____

DATE:_____ BELT RANK:_____

INSTRUCTOR:_____ WEIGHT:_____

TRAINING PARTNERS:_____

SESSION GOAL:_____

TECHNIQUE 1

_____
_____

TECHNIQUE 2

_____
_____

TECHNIQUE 3

_____
_____

NOTES

_____
_____

HOURS TRAINED:_____

DATE:_____ BELT RANK:_____

INSTRUCTOR:_____ WEIGHT:_____

TRAINING PARTNERS:_____

SESSION GOAL:_____

TECHNIQUE 1

_____

_____

TECHNIQUE 2

_____

_____

TECHNIQUE 3

_____

_____

NOTES

_____

_____

HOURS TRAINED:_____

DATE:_____ BELT RANK:_____

INSTRUCTOR:_____ WEIGHT:_____

TRAINING PARTNERS:_____

SESSION GOAL:_____

TECHNIQUE 1

_____

_____

TECHNIQUE 2

_____

_____

TECHNIQUE 3

_____

_____

NOTES

_____

_____

HOURS TRAINED:_____

DATE:_____ BELT RANK:_____

INSTRUCTOR:_____ WEIGHT:_____

TRAINING PARTNERS:_____

SESSION GOAL:_____

TECHNIQUE 1

_____
_____

TECHNIQUE 2

_____
_____

TECHNIQUE 3

_____
_____

NOTES

_____
_____

HOURS TRAINED:_____

DATE:_____ BELT RANK:_____

INSTRUCTOR:_____ WEIGHT:_____

TRAINING PARTNERS:_____

SESSION GOAL:_____

TECHNIQUE 1

_____

_____

TECHNIQUE 2

_____

_____

TECHNIQUE 3

_____

_____

NOTES

_____

_____

HOURS TRAINED:_____

DATE:_____ BELT RANK:_____

INSTRUCTOR:_____ WEIGHT:_____

TRAINING PARTNERS:_____

SESSION GOAL:_____

TECHNIQUE 1

_____
_____
_____

TECHNIQUE 2

_____
_____
_____

TECHNIQUE 3

_____
_____
_____

NOTES

_____
_____
_____

HOURS TRAINED:_____

DATE:_____ BELT RANK:_____

INSTRUCTOR:_____ WEIGHT:_____

TRAINING PARTNERS:_____

SESSION GOAL:_____

TECHNIQUE 1

_____
_____

TECHNIQUE 2

_____
_____

TECHNIQUE 3

_____
_____

NOTES

_____
_____

HOURS TRAINED:_____

DATE:_____ BELT RANK:_____

INSTRUCTOR:_____ WEIGHT:_____

TRAINING PARTNERS:_____

SESSION GOAL:_____

TECHNIQUE 1

_____

_____

TECHNIQUE 2

_____

_____

TECHNIQUE 3

_____

_____

NOTES

_____

_____

HOURS TRAINED:_____

DATE:_____ BELT RANK:_____

INSTRUCTOR:_____ WEIGHT:_____

TRAINING PARTNERS:_____

SESSION GOAL:_____

TECHNIQUE 1

_____

_____

TECHNIQUE 2

_____

_____

TECHNIQUE 3

_____

_____

NOTES

_____

_____

HOURS TRAINED:_____

DATE:_____ BELT RANK:_____

INSTRUCTOR:_____ WEIGHT:_____

TRAINING PARTNERS:_____

SESSION GOAL:_____

TECHNIQUE 1

_____

_____

TECHNIQUE 2

_____

_____

TECHNIQUE 3

_____

_____

NOTES

_____

_____

HOURS TRAINED:_____

DATE:_____ BELT RANK:_____

INSTRUCTOR:_____ WEIGHT:_____

TRAINING PARTNERS:_____

SESSION GOAL:_____

TECHNIQUE 1

_____

_____

TECHNIQUE 2

_____

_____

TECHNIQUE 3

_____

_____

NOTES

_____

_____

HOURS TRAINED:_____

DATE:_____ BELT RANK:_____

INSTRUCTOR:_____ WEIGHT:_____

TRAINING PARTNERS:_____

SESSION GOAL:_____

TECHNIQUE 1

_____
_____
_____

TECHNIQUE 2

_____
_____
_____

TECHNIQUE 3

_____
_____
_____

NOTES

_____
_____
_____

HOURS TRAINED:_____

DATE:_____ BELT RANK:_____

INSTRUCTOR:_____ WEIGHT:_____

TRAINING PARTNERS:_____

SESSION GOAL:_____

TECHNIQUE 1

_____

_____

TECHNIQUE 2

_____

_____

TECHNIQUE 3

_____

_____

NOTES

_____

_____

HOURS TRAINED:_____

DATE:_____ BELT RANK:_____

INSTRUCTOR:_____ WEIGHT:_____

TRAINING PARTNERS:_____

SESSION GOAL:_____

TECHNIQUE 1

_____

_____

TECHNIQUE 2

_____

_____

TECHNIQUE 3

_____

_____

NOTES

_____

_____

HOURS TRAINED:_____

DATE:_____ BELT RANK:_____

INSTRUCTOR:_____ WEIGHT:_____

TRAINING PARTNERS:_____

SESSION GOAL:_____

TECHNIQUE 1

_____

_____

TECHNIQUE 2

_____

_____

TECHNIQUE 3

_____

_____

NOTES

_____

_____

HOURS TRAINED:_____

DATE:_____ BELT RANK:_____

INSTRUCTOR:_____ WEIGHT:_____

TRAINING PARTNERS:_____

SESSION GOAL:_____

TECHNIQUE 1

_____
_____

TECHNIQUE 2

_____
_____

TECHNIQUE 3

_____
_____

NOTES

_____
_____

HOURS TRAINED:_____

DATE:_____ BELT RANK:_____

INSTRUCTOR:_____ WEIGHT:_____

TRAINING PARTNERS:_____

SESSION GOAL:_____

TECHNIQUE 1

_____

_____

TECHNIQUE 2

_____

_____

TECHNIQUE 3

_____

_____

NOTES

_____

_____

HOURS TRAINED:_____

DATE:_____ BELT RANK:_____

INSTRUCTOR:_____ WEIGHT:_____

TRAINING PARTNERS:_____

SESSION GOAL:_____

TECHNIQUE 1

_____
_____
_____

TECHNIQUE 2

_____
_____
_____

TECHNIQUE 3

_____
_____
_____

NOTES

_____
_____
_____

HOURS TRAINED:_____

DATE:_____ BELT RANK:_____

INSTRUCTOR:_____ WEIGHT:_____

TRAINING PARTNERS:_____

SESSION GOAL:_____

TECHNIQUE 1

_____

_____

TECHNIQUE 2

_____

_____

TECHNIQUE 3

_____

_____

NOTES

_____

_____

HOURS TRAINED:_____

DATE:_____ BELT RANK:_____

INSTRUCTOR:_____ WEIGHT:_____

TRAINING PARTNERS:_____

SESSION GOAL:_____

TECHNIQUE 1

_____

_____

TECHNIQUE 2

_____

_____

TECHNIQUE 3

_____

_____

NOTES

_____

_____

HOURS TRAINED:_____

DATE:_____ BELT RANK:_____

INSTRUCTOR:_____ WEIGHT:_____

TRAINING PARTNERS:_____

SESSION GOAL:_____

TECHNIQUE 1

_____
_____

TECHNIQUE 2

_____
_____

TECHNIQUE 3

_____
_____

NOTES

_____
_____

HOURS TRAINED:_____

DATE:_____ BELT RANK:_____

INSTRUCTOR:_____ WEIGHT:_____

TRAINING PARTNERS:_____

SESSION GOAL:_____

TECHNIQUE 1

_____

_____

TECHNIQUE 2

_____

_____

TECHNIQUE 3

_____

_____

NOTES

_____

_____

HOURS TRAINED:_____

Made in the USA
Las Vegas, NV
26 January 2024

84938136R00056